Seeing

A Troll Question Book™

By Kathie Billingslea Smith & Victoria Crenson
Illustrated by Robert S. Storms
Medical Consultant: Ira T. Fine, M.D.

Library of Congress Cataloging in Publication Data

Smith, Kathie Billingslea.
  Seeing.

  (A Troll question book)
  Summary: Answers a variety of questions about the
physical structure of the eye, how human beings and
animals see, and how to take care of our eyes.
  1. Vision—Juvenile literature. [1. Vision.
2. Questions and answers] I. Crenson, Victoria.
II. Storms, Robert S., ill. III. Title.
QP475.7.S64   1988   612'.8   87-5862
ISBN 0-8167-1008-2 (lib. bdg.)
ISBN 0-8167-1009-0 (pbk.)

Troll Associates
Mahwah, N.J.

To prove how important your eyes are, close them. Now try walking — carefully! Did you think it would be easy to walk? Imagine what it would be like to play, dress yourself, or eat without seeing.

Without stopping to think about it, you use your eyes in almost everything you do — choosing clothes to wear, riding a bike, looking at books, watching television, playing kickball.

my eyes?

Seeing tells you more about the world than any of your other senses — hearing, smelling, touching, or tasting.

Look at a ball. In a split second, your eyes can tell you that the ball is small, round, red, and on the floor. In the next instant, your eyes can give you a picture of the entire room.

The eyes send pictures to the brain every second they are open. All these pictures are stored in your memory. Most of the things you know you have learned by using your eyes.

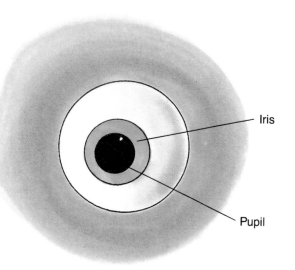

Iris

Pupil

Look at your eyes in a mirror. The large colored circle in each eye is called the *iris*. Irises can be different colors — blue, brown, green, or hazel.

In the middle of the iris, there is a small black circle called the

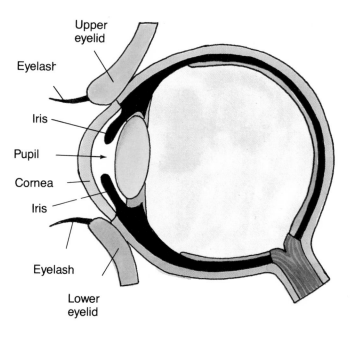

Upper eyelid

Eyelash

Iris

Pupil

Cornea

Iris

Eyelash

Lower eyelid

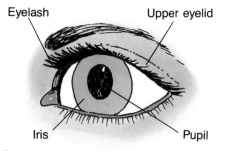

Eyelash

Upper eyelid

Iris

Pupil

Eyes are made up of many different parts that all work together to help you see. Eyes are shaped like balls, but you only see the front part of them.

pupil. It is really a hole that lets light into the eye. In bright light, the iris makes the pupil become smaller to protect the inside of the eye from too much light. When the light is dim, the iris makes the pupil get larger. This lets more light into the eye to help you see better. The iris in a camera lens works exactly the same way to let the right amount of light into the film.

On top of the iris and pupil is a clear covering called the *cornea*. It is like a window that lets light pass to the inside of the eye.

Eyelids and eyelashes are important parts of eyes, too. They help protect them from dust and too much light. Also, each time you blink, your eyelids spread small tears over your eyes to keep them moist.

How do I see?

Look at a tree. Light is reflected from the tree back to your eyes. The light goes through the pupil to a *lens* behind the iris. This lens changes its shape and focuses the light from the tree onto the *retina* at the back of the eye.

The retina is a little bit like a movie screen, only the picture projected on it is upside down and backwards!

Nerves in the retina carry a message of this picture to a certain part of the brain. Here the picture is turned right side

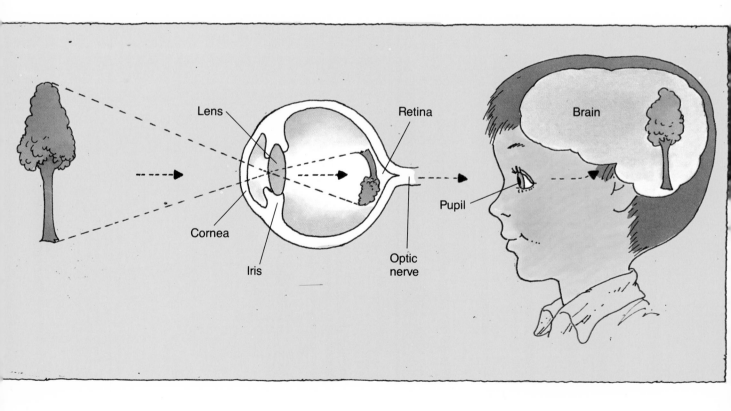

Lens

Retina

Brain

Cornea

Pupil

Iris

Optic nerve

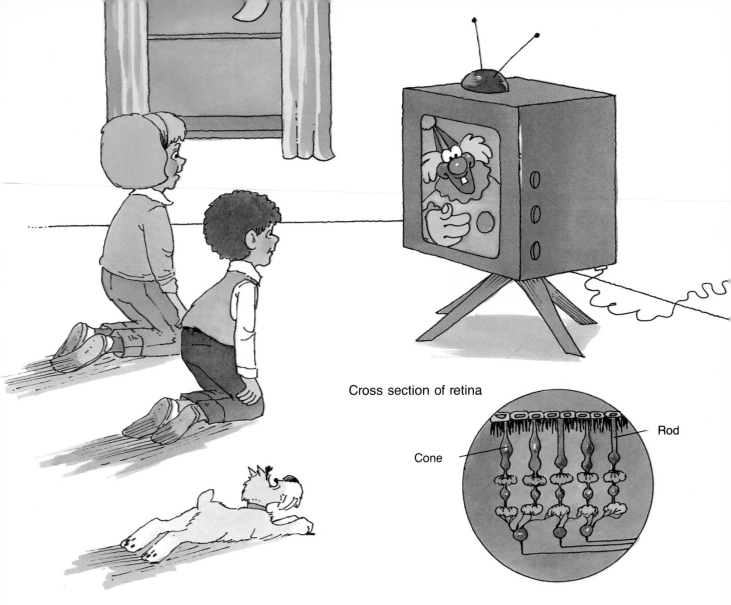

Cross section of retina

Rod

Cone

up so that the tree is seen correctly.

The retina has layers of tightly packed cells called *rods* and *cones*. Rods are very sensitive to light. They help you see at night. Cones need light to work. They allow you to see colors.

All colors come from light. That is why at night, when it is dark, you see only black. The cones in your eyes do not have enough light to work and let you see colors.

colors?

Light looks clear, but it is really a mixture of different colored lights. When light shines on a red ball, most of the colors in the light are absorbed by the ball. The red light is reflected back to your eyes. That is the color you see. A blue sofa reflects blue light. Orange pumpkins reflect orange light.

You can see the hidden colors in light when you shine light through a *prism*. A prism is a triangular piece of glass. When light shines through a prism, the prism bends the light and splits it up into a display of colors.

Raindrops can act just like a prism. The sun shines through the raindrops, and the sunlight is split into all the colors of . . . a rainbow!

Which color is your favorite?

All kinds of animals use their eyes to learn best how to live in their surroundings. Most animals have eyes that are suited to their needs.

Owls, which are nocturnal birds that hunt at night, can see very well in the dark. In almost total blackness, an owl can see

and pounce on a mouse that is six feet away.

Other birds that migrate long distances look at the sun, moon, and stars to help guide them when flying.

Houseflies have eyes that enable them to see on all sides of their bodies at the same time. (That is why it is so hard to catch them!)

animals see?

The animals with the best eyesight are birds of prey, such as hawks, eagles, and falcons. An eagle flying in the air can see a rabbit that is about one-and-a-half miles away! These

birds can see eight to ten times better than people can!

Many animals can only see in black and white. Other animals can see only a few colors. Frogs can see blue, and bees can see all colors except red. Chimpanzees can see all of the colors that people can.

What are tears?

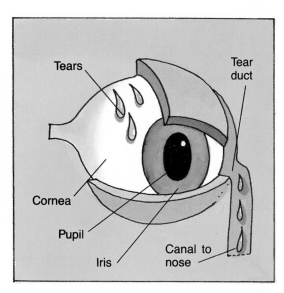

Tears

Tear duct

Cornea

Pupil

Iris

Canal to nose

Eyes need protection from dust and smoke in the air. So every time an eye blinks, it gets a bath! Special glands above each eye make a fluid that is squeezed out whenever the eye blinks. The fluid flows over the eyeball to wash it. Then the fluid drains through the *tear duct* located at the corner of each eye into the top of the nose.

When you are sad or something makes your eyes sting, the glands make more fluid. The tube cannot drain fast enough. It overflows and tears run down your cheeks.

Taste a tear — it is salty. Besides salt, a tear contains a germ killer and a lubricant so the eyelid can slide easily over the eyeball.

Because eyes are such important parts of the body, they need very special care.

Be careful when using sharp, pointed objects such as sticks, pencils, paintbrushes, or scissors. Keep them away from your eyes!

When reading or playing, make sure there is plenty of light to help you see well. But don't ever look directly into the sun. This could be very harmful.

If a little piece of dirt gets into your eye, do not try to rub

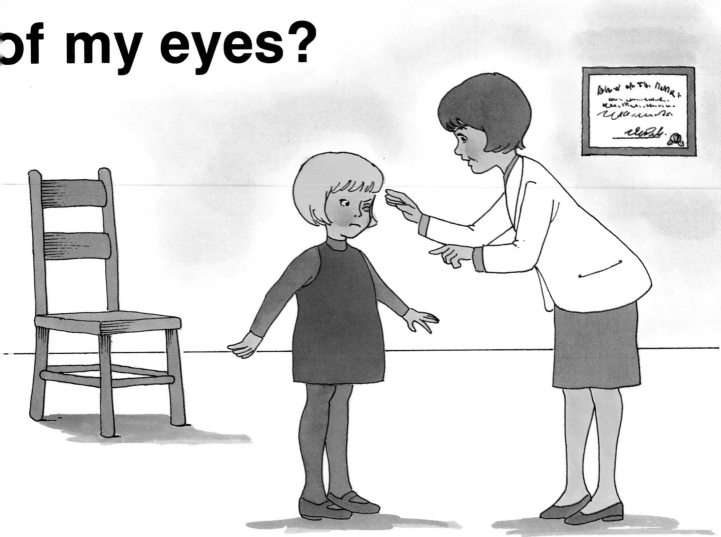

it out. This might scar the cornea or put germs into the eye. It is better to see if your tears will wash it out. If that does not happen, your parents or a teacher can gently rinse your eye with clear water.

Sometimes eyes do not work as well as they should. Things you look at might appear fuzzy or blurry. If you have trouble seeing clearly, a doctor should examine your eyes to find the problem. It's a good idea to have your eyes checked once a year anyway.

What happens when

A doctor called an *optometrist* or an *ophthalmologist* examines your eyes.

The doctor may ask you to look at a chart with rows of letters. At the top of the chart is a big letter E. The next row has several letters, smaller than the E, but all the same size. Every other row of letters is smaller than the row before. The doctor asks you to keep reading until you can no longer see letters on the chart. This shows the doctor the condition of your eyes.

FZDMO

get my eyes examined?

Often the doctor puts special drops in your eyes. These drops make the pupils *dilate*, or grow larger. Then the doctor looks through the pupils to see the insides of your eyes. An instrument called an *ophthalmoscope* helps the doctor to see the cornea, lens, and retina. With this tool, the doctor checks to see if your eyes are healthy. Have your eyes checked by the doctor regularly.

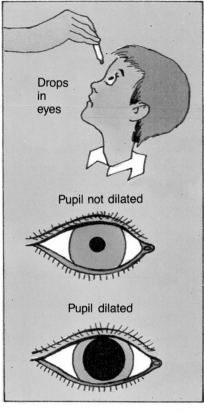

Drops in eyes

Pupil not dilated

Pupil dilated

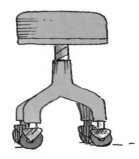

Who needs glasses?

Some people need glasses when they have trouble seeing things that are either close or far away. The lenses in their eyes are not shaped correctly to make clear pictures on their retinas.

A person who is *nearsighted* can clearly see things close up, but faraway objects look fuzzy to him. *Farsighted* people can see things in the distance but cannot clearly see nearby objects.

Farsighted   Corrected

Nearsighted   Corrected

Lenses for correction

Like an out-of-focus movie projector, the lenses of a nearsighted person focus the picture in front of the movie screen or retina. The farsighted person has lenses that focus the picture behind the retina.

Eye doctors examine and test these people's eyes. Then they fit the people with glasses. The glasses have special lenses that help them see clearly again.

Some people wear contact lenses. These plastic lenses are so small that they are worn right on the corneas of the eyes!

Does someone in your family wear glasses or contact lenses?

Can everyone see?

A blind person is one who cannot see. Some people are partially blind and can only see a little. They cannot watch television or see snowflakes or drive a car. Blind people must find new ways to do things without using their eyes.

It is hard for blind people to walk around when they cannot see where they are going. Some blind people walk alone and use canes to help them "feel" their way. They sometimes memorize how many steps it takes to get from one place to another. Some blind people have specially trained dogs, called Seeing Eye dogs, to help guide them.

Blind people cannot see words to read books. Instead, they learn to read with their hands! They use a special alphabet called *Braille*. Each letter of this alphabet is a different pattern of little dots or bumps that stick up on the pages of Braille books. Blind people know what each pattern of bumps means. They move their fingers over the bumps and read by feeling the Braille letters.

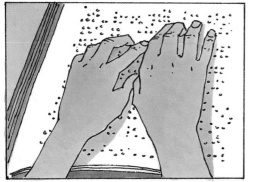

These are the patterns of dots that make up the Braille alphabet:

How would you write your name in Braille?

a	b	c	d	e	f	g
h	i	j	k	l	m	n
o	p	q	r	s	t	u
v	w	x	y	z		

Optical illusions are pictures that play tricks on the eyes. When you look at an optical illusion, your brain doesn't quite know what to think because the picture doesn't seem to make sense.

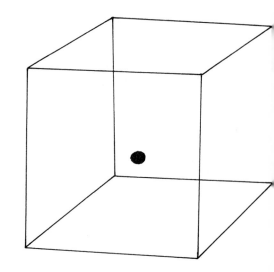

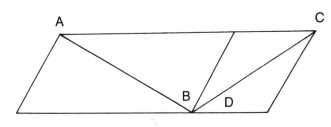

In the drawing above, lines AB and CD are really the *same* length.

Look at this picture. It is an optical illusion.

Is the dot at the front of the cube or at the back of the cube?

In the drawings to the right, both long lines are the same length.

llusions?

Try this one. Look carefully at the picture. What do you see?

Do you see a candlestick holder? — or two faces? Sometimes you can look at an object and see more than one thing!

Eyes help you see things, but the brain helps you understand what you see.

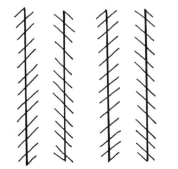

The vertical lines are parallel to each other.

This hat is no taller than it is wide.

How can I see more?

By really looking! The more carefully you use your eyes, the more you will see and learn.

Now look at a tree. A tree is not *just* a tree. It has a trunk growing out of the ground with bark of a certain color. A tree has branches covered with leaves — each one slightly different from the other. A tree is a home for animals. Maybe you see some of them — a family of birds, cocoons with caterpillars inside waiting to become butterflies, squirrels leaping from branch to branch.

By practicing, you can teach your eyes to notice more about the world.

Seeing is especially important for painters, photographers, and other visual artists. By looking closely at everything, artists find what they need to imagine and create wonderful treats for *our* eyes.